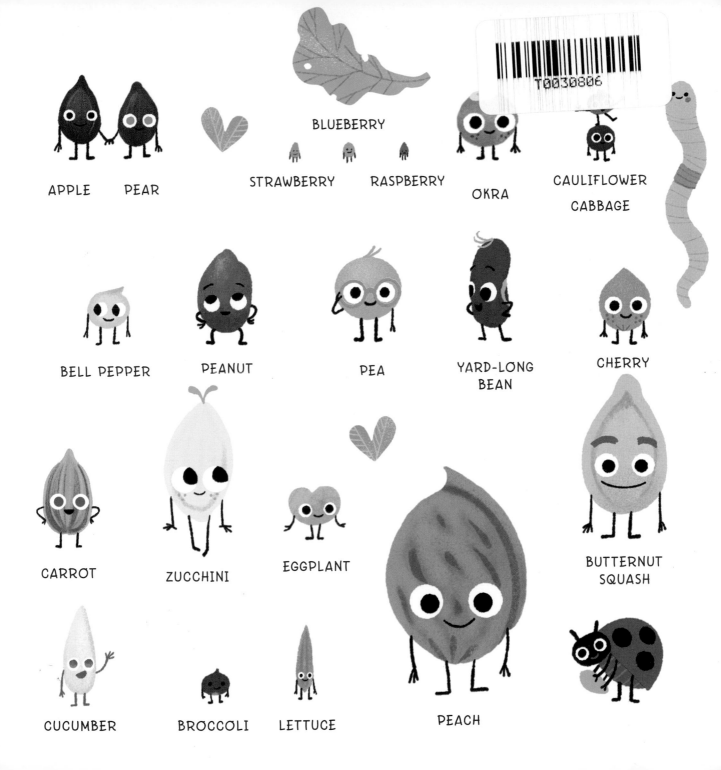

APPLE   PEAR

BLUEBERRY

STRAWBERRY   RASPBERRY   OKRA

CAULIFLOWER
CABBAGE

BELL PEPPER   PEANUT   PEA   YARD-LONG
BEAN

CHERRY

CARROT   ZUCCHINI   EGGPLANT

BUTTERNUT
SQUASH

CUCUMBER   BROCCOLI   LETTUCE   PEACH

For Liina—life is full of wonder.
Stay curious.

Joyful Books for Curious Minds

An imprint of Macmillan Children's Publishing Group, LLC
Odd Dot® is a registered trademark of Macmillan Publishing Group, LLC
120 Broadway, New York, NY 10271 • OddDot.com • mackids.com

EDITOR Julia Sooy
DESIGNER Tim Hall
PRODUCTION EDITORS Jennifer Healey & Hayley O'Brion
PRODUCTION MANAGERS Barbara Cho & Jocelyn O'Dowd
TITLE LETTERING Mirka Hokkanen

ISBN 978-1-250-88560-9
Library of Congress Control Number 2023937967

Our books may be purchased in bulk for promotional, educational, or business use.
Please contact your local bookseller or the Macmillan Corporate and Premium Sales Department
at (800) 221-7945 ext. 5442 or by email at MacmillanSpecialMarkets@macmillan.com.

First edition, 2024
Printed in China by RR Donnelley Asia Printing Solutions Ltd., Dongguan City, Guangdong Province

1 3 5 7 9 10 8 6 4 2

LITTLE SEASONS
SPRING SEEDS

MIRKA HOKKANEN

odd dot

New York

Winter is a quiet time in the backyard.

Seeds on the ground are peacefully sleeping,
waiting for spring.

When spring arrives, the weather warms and we get more sun. It's the perfect time for seeds to wake up.

A garden or your backyard is a great place to watch seeds grow.

You can plant many kinds
of seeds in a garden.

Some are so tiny, you
could easily lose them.

And some are as big as your fist!

When you plant seeds in your garden and give them water, they start to grow roots.

SLURP!

Roots are like straws that seeds use to take in food and water.

When seeds eat enough, they start to grow shoots that sprout into leaves.

The leaves soak up energy from the sun, making the plants healthy and green.

Look at those sprouts!

Different seeds grow into different plants,
which produce different fruits and vegetables.

peaches

broccoli

beans

peas

When plants grow up, they can make seeds of their own. You can find seeds on the outside...

or on the inside.

Some plants have flowers
that make a lot of seeds!

pumpkins   watermelon   zucchini

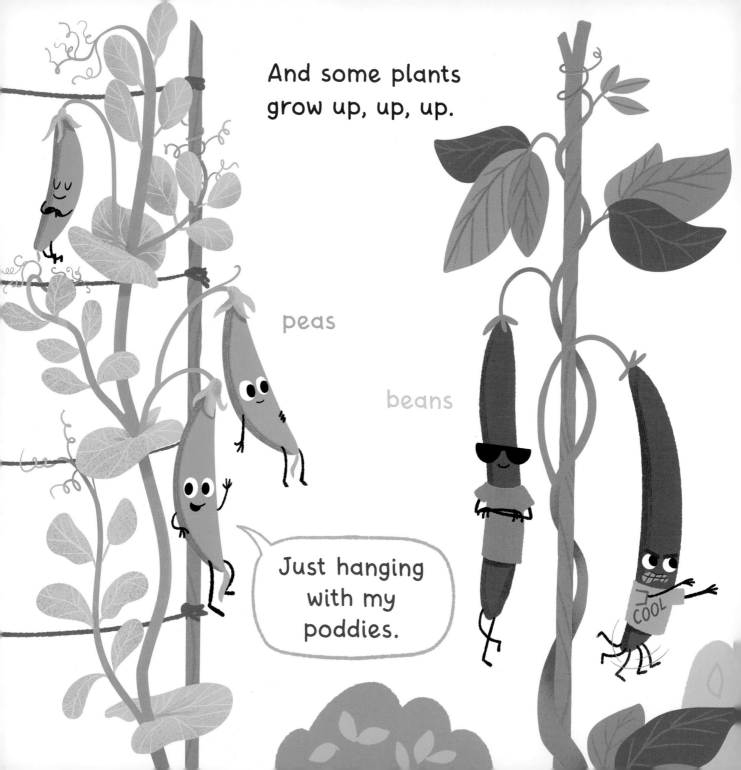

Pbbtt!

raspberries

Seeds are important because they grow into healthy fruits, vegetables, and all kinds of plants!

Sometimes you eat the seeds instead of planting them.

Whether you plant them or eat them,
seeds are really important.

A CLOSER LOOK AT SEEDS

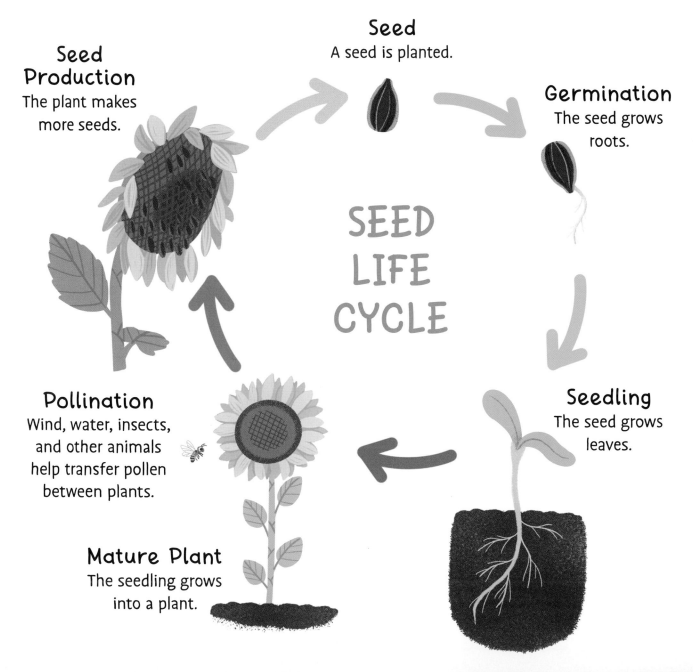

Seed
A seed is planted.

Germination
The seed grows roots.

Seed Production
The plant makes more seeds.

SEED LIFE CYCLE

Seedling
The seed grows leaves.

Pollination
Wind, water, insects, and other animals help transfer pollen between plants.

Mature Plant
The seedling grows into a plant.

TIME TO GROW

A seed needs sun, water, and soil to grow big and strong.

Ready for winter.

PARTS OF A SEED

Seed Coat
The seed coat protects the baby plant inside.

Embryo
The embryo contains the leaves, stem, and root that make up the baby plant.

Food Storage
The food storage provides nutrients for the seed to start growing.

START YOUR OWN SEEDS

If you want to feel connected to the earth, try growing seeds!
Here's what you'll need:

- a quart-size sealable plastic bag or clean glass jar
- beans (most dry beans should work)
- cotton balls
- water
- sunlight

Have a grown-up print out the free downloadable growth chart at mirkah.com/books

Wet a handful of cotton balls and place them in your bag or jar. They should be wet but not dripping.

Place one to three beans an inch or so apart on the cotton balls. Put your container by a window. If using a bag, seal it.

Wait and observe. Can you predict what will happen the next day? Keep a growth chart to track the beans' progress.

If the cotton balls dry out, carefully add some water to them.

GROW DEEPER

What do seeds need to grow? What happens if the beans do not get sunlight or water?

You can make more bean containers to find out. Let one container dry out by the window; put another in a dark place but keep it moist. Then compare the seeds every week.

⭐ For a fun variation, try starting parsley, dill, or lettuce seeds in the spring with moist cotton balls, then transfer the seedlings into pots with soil or into a garden bed. If you keep your growing seedlings indoors, make sure they get plenty of sunlight.

EXPLORE THE OUTDOORS

As you walk around outside, observe seeds you find and guess where they came from or what they might grow into. Watch for dandelions, grasses, acorns, pine cones, and maple seeds.

Maple seeds make neat helicopters when you drop them from high up. Fresh ones can be split apart at the seed and stuck to the tip of your nose for a funny moment.

Seeds in nature provide food for many animals. Animals that eat seeds are called granivores. Ants, bean weevils, crickets, mice, squirrels, chipmunks, rabbits, finches, blackbirds, woodpeckers, raccoons, and deer are all granivores.

Ready for takeoff!

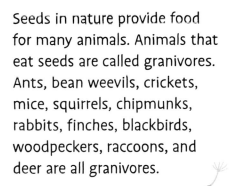

Shoo, you furry beast!

TASTE TEST

There are so many different fruits and vegetables! Some are sour and some are sweet. Some are crunchy and some are mushy. How many have you tasted? What was the last one you tried? Point to the face that looks like the one you made when you first tasted it. Can you pick a new fruit or vegetable to try next?

Before eating fruits and vegetables, help your grown-up wash them. Look closely. Can you find any seeds?

Use the free downloadable chart at mirkah.com/books to keep track of all the new foods you have tried and how they taste.

| Avocado | Pepper | Tomato | Cherry | Pea |
| Carrot | Lettuce | Eggplant | Lemon | Peach |

Apple

Pear

Broccoli

Starfruit

Cauliflower

Orange

Cantaloupe

Green bean

Plum

Blackberry

Cucumber

Cabbage

Strawberry

Blueberry

Grape

Zucchini

Radish

Watermelon

Pomegranate

Kiwi

Pineapple

Okra

Persimmon

GROW DEEPER

If you ate a lot of beets, blackberries, or carrots, did you notice anything different when you went to the bathroom?

LEARNING WITH SEEDS

Seeds are perfect for sorting, counting, practicing math, and exploring patterns.

What seeds can you find in the kitchen? Look for popcorn, rice, sunflower seeds, and snack nuts. You might even have a bag of mixed dry beans meant for soup!

SORTING

Have a grown-up mix different types of seeds in a bowl. Then try sorting them by type. You can make piles or sort them into cups or circles drawn on paper. You could even set up a sorting game by taping paper towel rolls flat against the side of a box or cabinet. Place cups below, then drop the seeds through the tubes into the cups. How many can you get in each cup? How many didn't make it? Did you mix any up?

MATH

Have a grown-up draw five circles that get bigger and bigger on a piece of paper and label them 1 to 5, smallest to biggest. Can you place the right amount of seeds in each circle? Try adding the number of seeds in the different circles together: Pick up the seeds from circle 2 and circle 3 and hold them all in your hand. How many seeds do you have? Pick up the seeds from circle 5 and add them to the ones already in your hand. How many do you have now? You just practiced addition! Now put two seeds back in circle 2. How many seeds are left in your hand? You just practiced subtraction!

Use the free downloadable resources at mirkah.com/books to print out math and sorting worksheets.

SEED ART AND MUSIC

Because seeds come in so many colors and sizes, they are perfect for art activities!

Glue seeds in a row to create curious caterpillars. Use glue, seeds, and crayons to create people or animal faces on paper plates. Or cut out animal shapes from cardboard or paper plates and decorate them with seeds, creating fun patterns.

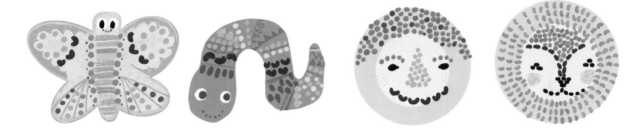

Create musical maracas with seeds in containers. Use any type of unbreakable container that you can seal tightly and shake with one hand: plastic eggs, plastic spoons taped together, empty containers with lids, or toilet paper rolls with the ends folded in. Add one type of seed to one container and another type to a different container, leaving plenty of room for the seeds to move around. You can also try putting more seeds in one container than in another. Have a grown-up help you close and seal the containers with tape or glue to keep the seeds inside. Shake each of your maracas. Do the different types and amounts of seeds change the sound? Which do you like best?

On the next page you will find a matching and memory game! Tear out the page and separate it into cards along the perforated lines.

High five, partner.

PISTACHIO   ONION   FIG   RADISH   APPLE

CORN   SPINACH   GREEN BEAN   TOMATO   AVOCADO

WATERMELON   LEMON   PLUM   SUNFLOWER   CANTALOUPE

Peach

Peach

Apple

Apple

Tomato

Tomato

Cucumber

Cucumber

Pea

Pea

Radish

Radish